To:

Love,

All You Need is Love

Coloring Card
Sandy Mahony
Mary Lou Brown

Great happiness
and love
to you!

TONIGHT
We Dance
UNDER THE
Stars

Happy Valentine's day

YOU
AND
ME

LOVE
DOES NOT
MAKE THE WORLD
GO ROUND...LOVE IS
WHAT MAKES THE
RIDE WORTHWHILE.

adventurelearningpress.com

www.ingramcont
Lightning Source
Chambersburg PA
CBHW07201528
45788CB000

* 9 7 8 1